TAROT *of* COCKTAILS

Here's to good libations and good vibrations.

TAROT *of* COCKTAILS

Katy Seibel

Andrews McMeel
PUBLISHING®

CONTENTS

INITIATION AND BACKGROUND vii

TOOLS ix

INGREDIENTS AND TECHNIQUES xii

A FINAL NOTE xvi

RECIPES xvi

BLOOD AND SMOKE 3

THE HERBALIST 4

RULE OF THREE 7

THE MILKY MOON 8

THE STRAW MAN 11

THE GRAIL 12

QUEEN OF BEES 15

SPICE OF LIFE 16

PITH OF STICKS 19

PRINCESS OF MOSCOW 20

THE ARCHER 23

THE FEAST 24

ROOT OF ALL 27

THE FIRST MAN 28

THE ELDER 31

THE TRIPLE CROWN 32

ARC OF TIME 35

BREAK OF DAWN 36

THE CLIMBING VINE 39

THE WHITE ELEPHANT 40

THE BLACK NIGHT 43

THE VIOLET TWILIGHT 44

THE SUNDIAL 47

WINTER'S PEAK 48

NEW BEGINNING 51

THE GOLD STANDARD 52

THE MAGIC BREW 55

FLOWER OF PALMS 56

SEER OF DREAMS 59

THE BITTER TRUTH 60

NECTAR OF THE GODS 63

THE BELL TOWER 64

THE FIRST BLUSH 67

MONK OF THE MOUNTAINS 68

THE TRIFECTA 71

THE MIRAGE 72

THE FLOWER CROWN 75

THE CALYPSO 76

THE ROSE-COLORED GLASS 79

SWEET SURRENDER 80

CITY OF EMERALD 83

THE POINTED LEAF 84

MILK OF GOLD 87

THE HEDGE MAZE 88

THE LAMB'S TAIL 91

INDEX 94

INITIATION

As the bearer of this book, you are most fortunate—there are many fine cocktails in your future. While the spirit of classic tarot cards dwells within the pages that follow, we'll delve into divine drinks more than divination. This faithful companion will help you master the alchemy of alcohol and the magic of mixology. I will begin with a bit of history, followed by a quick apprenticeship on the art of home bartending, including essential tools and trusted techniques. Then, the heart of the matter—a library of libations with flavor profiles to please every palate. There are playful spiked floats, like Princess of Moscow (page 20) and Seer of Dreams (page 59), that are easy to drink and easy to make. For the more adventurous and ambitious, I offer herbaceous earthly delights, like The Bell Tower (page 64), The Herbalist (page 4), and City of Emerald (page 83). If you prefer to feel the bite of your booze, I present spirit-forward sippers like The Climbing Vine (page 39), The Mirage (page 72), and Monk of the Mountains (page 68). This is just a taste of the spellbinding drinks you'll discover.

The potable potions contained herein are sure to tantalize your taste buds and lift your spirits. I hope you savor every sip of your journey through *Tarot of Cocktails*.

BACKGROUND

Originally developed as playing cards in 14th-century Europe, tarot was adapted for divinatory use as early as the 18th century. From facing the day to starting a new journey, individuals turn to tarot for mundane conundrums, cosmic questions, and everything in between.

The well-known and well-loved Rider-Waite-Smith deck served as inspiration for the original illustrations in this book. A collaboration between academic mystic A.E. Waite and artist Pamela Colman Smith, it was originally published by the Rider Company in 1910. Its iconic art is widely recognizable—saturated colors, eye-catching compositions, deceptively simple line work. From the harrowing terror of The Tower to the blithe levity of The Fool, I've long been enraptured by the beauty of Smith's art. To create my illustrations, I reimagined the cards to coincide with cocktail recipes—pentacles become citrus wheels, cinnamon sticks stand in for wands, and so on.

Alcohol, like tarot, has a long and significant history in the human narrative. People have been making and enjoying fermented beverages since ancient times. Drinking can be social, celebratory, even sacramental. Classic cocktails have experienced a resurgence in recent decades, and the craft has reached new echelons of artistry. The recipes ahead strike a nice balance—interesting enough to intrigue seasoned bartenders, yet accessible to more amateur enthusiasts.

Like a spread of tarot cards, a cocktail combines different components—each with a unique role to play, a flavor or texture to contribute—and that purpose changes depending on the combination and quantities of ingredients. The ritual involves certain instruments, careful measurements, an alchemy of ingredients, and an order of operations. There's a science to it, but there's magic in the mix, too.

With this book, I wish to provide a beautiful artifact to please the eye, a practical tool to educate and inform, and an opportunity to discover the magic of cocktails. Whether you're a wise witch or know nothing of tarot . . . whether you're a veteran bartender or have never made more than a gin and tonic . . . this book has something for all. Now let's raise a glass to good fortune and good drinks.

TOOLS

JIGGER

Jiggers are used to measure the volume of ingredients. Precise measurements are of utmost importance as even small discrepancies in ingredient quantities can upset the balance of a cocktail. Jiggers are typically hourglass-shaped with different measurements on either side and sometimes additional increments etched inside the cups. Find the one that best suits you, or collect multiple jiggers to keep on hand. Tip: The smallest quantity (in ounces) in the recipes that follow is ¼. If your jigger doesn't have an increment for this measurement, take note that ¼ ounce equals 1½ teaspoons.

SHAKER

Most of the drinks in the book are shaken, so this will be a workhorse tool. Shaking serves to chill, dilute, mix, and aerate a cocktail. There are a few different varieties of shakers, the most common being the cobbler shaker and the Boston shaker. The three-piece cobbler features a metal tin, a top with a built-in strainer, and a cap. The two-piece Boston consists of a pint glass that fits into a larger metal tin.

cobbler shaker

jigger

boston shaker

MIXING GLASS

This vessel is designed for drinks that are stirred rather than shaken. They are typically made of glass, feature a spout for easy pouring, and require a separate strainer. You can opt for a glass designed specifically for this purpose, or you can use the tumbler portion of your cocktail shaker or a pint glass for stirring.

BARSPOON

The barspoon is your go-to tool for stirred drinks. Its length accommodates a variety of mixing glass sizes, and its twisted shape allows it to spin freely as it moves around the edge of the glass.

STRAINER

Strainers prevent ice and other solids from falling into your final drink. Hawthorne strainers have a spring around the edge to create a snug fit and catch muddled ingredients. Even if you're using a cobbler shaker with a built-in strainer, I recommend having a Hawthorne strainer on hand—they work a lot better. Some drinks, such as those containing muddled fruits or herbs, call for double-straining through a fine-mesh sieve, so you'll want to have one handy. The simple and classic julep strainer, a shallow perforated bowl with a handle, is ideal for stirred drinks. Select one that fits snugly in your mixing glass of choice.

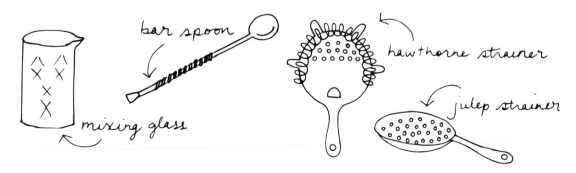

bar spoon

hawthorne strainer

julep strainer

mixing glass

MUDDLER

A muddler is a tool made of metal or wood that is used to mash fruits and herbs to release their juices and flavors.

GLASSWARE

There are many additional types of glasses that aren't mentioned here, but these are the primary ones used for my recipes.

Coupe: This stemmed bowl-shaped glass is the go-to for cocktails served up (without ice). The stem allows you to hold your drink without warming it up.

Lowball: Also known as a rocks glass or an old-fashioned glass, the lowball is a short, wide tumbler for drinks served on the rocks or with a single large cube.

Highball: Taller and narrower than a lowball, the highball is ideal for drinks served on the rocks with a mixer, such as soda. The Collins glass is similar to the highball and can be used in its place.

muddler

fine-mesh sieve

highball glass

lowball glass

coupe glass

INGREDIENTS and TECHNIQUES

ICE

Ice is the cornerstone of the cocktail—even drinks served up need to get cold first. While standard ice cubes work just fine, perfect one-inch cubes create particularly attractive drinks. Some of the cocktails in the book call for a single big cube, which can be created with a two-inch mold. Large cubes melt slower to keep drinks chilled while minimizing dilution. These are ideal for spirit-forward sipping drinks like an old fashioned. Only one drink in the deck, my take on a mint julep, calls for crushed ice. Unless you own a refrigerator that produces crushed ice, you can pulse regular ice in a blender or place it in a clean cloth bag or smooth towel and (cautiously, of course) smash it with a wooden mallet or other blunt kitchen tool.

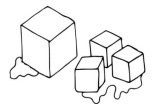 

LIQUEURS

Liqueurs can be expensive. Since recipes usually call for small quantities, a single bottle should last a long while on your home bar. And they're expensive for a reason. There's often a complex—and even secret—art to their production, and they add undeniable depth and interest to cocktails. That said, if you don't see yourself ever using an entire bottle of, say, Chartreuse, or you'd like to sample it before you commit to a full bottle, ask your liquor store if they carry it in a pint or miniature size.

SIMPLE SYRUP

Simple syrup is the easiest way to incorporate neutral sweetness into a drink. Liqueurs and other sweeteners (like honey and maple syrup) add their own distinct flavor, and granulated sugar doesn't dissolve in cold drinks. Simple syrup combines seamlessly with other liquids, and the aptly named ingredient is indeed quite simple to make. Also, as you'll soon see, you can infuse your syrup with fruits, herbs, or spices to create your own unique sweeteners.

Technique

Combine equal parts sugar and water in a saucepan over medium heat, stirring until the sugar has dissolved completely. Remove from the heat and let cool before using. Keep refrigerated in a covered container for up to 1 month.

GARNISHES

Although a garnish is sometimes just a pretty finishing touch, it can also serve an important purpose. For example, a citrus wedge encourages the drinker to increase the tartness of the beverage to taste. A citrus wheel lends aroma and a more subtle infusion of flavor. A twist releases fragrant oils that enhance the profile of the drink. A salt rim adds a whole new layer of flavor.

Citrus Twist: To create a citrus twist, use either a vegetable peeler or a paring knife. After washing your fruit with water, remove a swath of zest while cutting into the white pith as little as possible. Squeeze the peel above your drink to release a mist of oil, then gently rub it along the rim of the glass before placing it atop the drink, or discard it if you prefer not to further infuse your cocktail with the essence of citrus.

Salt Rim: Swipe the outside rim of your glass with a citrus fruit or water, just enough to slightly wet it. Roll it in coarse salt on a flat surface such as a plate. Shake off any excess salt and discard any salt that has fallen inside the glass. If you don't like salt with every sip or want to give your guests both options, dip one side of your rim and leave the rest bare.

Slapped Herbs: You'll notice that some recipes call for a "slapped" herb as a garnish. This simply means that, before placing the herb in your final drink, you slap it against your hand (or clap it between them) to release its fragrance and subtle hints of flavor.

EGG WHITES

Thanks to effective public health warnings, many people are put off by the thought of consuming raw egg white. That said, classic cocktails often called for albumen, and it's a commonplace ingredient at modern craft cocktail bars. Only two of the recipes ahead contain egg white. Leave it out if you prefer, take extra precautions, and consume at your own risk—but the creamy texture of an egg white cocktail is truly divine. Here are some tips:

1. If you want to play it extra safe, you can wash the shell first and avoid using the shell to separate the yolk, as that can introduce bacteria. Also, use good-quality (organic, local) eggs if possible.

2. To separate an egg, crack it into a bowl and use a spoon to gently remove the yolk.

3. To properly emulsify and integrate the egg white, dry shake (without ice) until your arm aches before adding ice and giving it another really good shake.

SHAKEN OR STIRRED?

Generally, any drink that includes non-spirit ingredients (fruit juice, syrup, egg white, dairy) should be shaken. This ensures that the ingredients are fully integrated and produces a more frothy texture. Carbonated ingredients should be added at the end of the process—never shaken. If a drink is served on the rocks, use fresh ice for the final presentation of the cocktail.

A drink that contains only spirits, such as a martini, is usually stirred with ice until chilled. This prevents aeration and results in a smooth texture. For drinks that are served up, I recommend chilling your glass. This can be achieved by filling a glass with ice water until cold or storing glasses in the freezer until ready for use.

A FINAL NOTE

While it's always admirable to strive for an ideal, you needn't do so at the expense of your enjoyment. Shortcuts for the sake of convenience or simplicity are welcome. A bag of ice from the gas station instead of perfect gleaming cubes; bottled juice standing in for fresh-squeezed; a jelly jar in lieu of a coupe glass; or a wooden spoon acting as a muddler are perfectly good substitutes. Find what works for you, so you can find joy in the ritual of drink.

RECIPES

Now that you have a sturdy foundation of fundamental tools, ingredients, and techniques, the time is nigh—nay, the moment has arrived. You're ready to begin mixing up some magic. You may start from the beginning and proceed along a linear path, or perhaps you prefer to hop around. If so, glance through the recipes to see what speaks to you— ingredients, flavors, art, or words. You can even leave it in the hands of fate and open to a random page. All the recipes in this book are made to serve one, but don't let that stop you from making more. I hope you share the love with those you love.

Which cocktail will you conjure first?

TAROT *of* COCKTAILS

BLOOD and SMOKE.

BLOOD AND SMOKE

Blood and Smoke, a remix of the classic Blood and Sand, swaps Scotch for mezcal, an agave-based spirit with distinctive smoky notes. The bright blood orange, sweet yet sharp maraschino liqueur, and crisp dry vermouth balance out the dominant smokiness of the profile. As you enjoy, take a moment to ruminate on a deep thought.

Tip: Regular fresh orange juice can be used in place of blood orange juice.

INGREDIENTS

1½ ounces mezcal
1 ounce fresh blood orange juice
½ ounce dry vermouth
½ ounce maraschino liqueur

Garnish
Blood orange twist

TECHNIQUE

Shake the mezcal, juice, vermouth, and liqueur with ice for several seconds, until chilled. Strain into a chilled coupe glass. Garnish with the blood orange twist.

THE HERBALIST

Light and refreshing while packing a powerful punch of flavor, The Herbalist is a dynamic beer cocktail. Sage, IPA, and gin form an herbaceous, slightly bitter foundation, while pineapple lifts and sweetens the profile and adds a delightfully frothy texture. As you enjoy, pay a little homage to the power of plants.

Tip: To make fresh pineapple juice, muddle cubed pineapple until all large chunks are eliminated, then strain through a fine-mesh sieve.

INGREDIENTS

2 sage leaves
¼ ounce Simple Syrup (page xi)
2 ounces pineapple juice
1 ounce dry gin
2 ounces IPA

Garnish
Slapped sage leaves

TECHNIQUE

Gently muddle the sage leaves and syrup in your shaker. Add the juice and gin, then shake with ice for several seconds, until chilled. Strain through a fine-mesh sieve into a highball glass filled with ice. Top with the IPA and gently stir. Garnish with the slapped sage leaves.

THE HERBALIST.

RULE OF THREE

Rule of Three falls somewhere between a sweet tea and a whiskey smash with refreshing mint, juicy peach, and an unexpected hint of smoke. As you enjoy, focus on finding balance, and don't be afraid to make your own rules.

Tip: Lapsang souchong is a Chinese smoke-dried black tea. None on hand? You can use regular black tea as a substitute.

INGREDIENTS

Small handful of mint leaves
1 lemon wedge
1½ ounces bourbon
½ ounce peach liqueur
½ ounce Smoked Black Tea Concentrate (see below)

Garnish
Grilled lemon wheel

TECHNIQUE

Muddle the mint and lemon wedge in your shaker. Add the bourbon, liqueur, and tea concentrate, then shake with ice for several seconds, until chilled. Strain into a lowball glass filled with ice. Garnish with the grilled lemon wheel.

SMOKED BLACK TEA CONCENTRATE
Makes 1 cup

Steep 4 teaspoons or 4 bags lapsang souchong tea in 1 cup boiling water for 10 minutes. Strain the leaves or discard the bags. Let cool before using. Keep refrigerated in a covered container for 3 to 5 days.

RULE ᴏꜰ THREE.

THE MILKY MOON

Calming and familiar with an air of the afar, this take on a classic milk punch draws influence from masala chai. The black tea, spices, and milk make for a rich, creamy cocktail, while the cold temperature lightens things up. As you enjoy, look to the bright beacon above as a source of serenity.

INGREDIENTS

2 ounces whole milk (or milk alternative)
3 ounces chai tea concentrate
1½ ounces gold rum
Pinch of ground cardamom
Small pinch of salt
Small pinch of ground black pepper

Garnish
Star anise

TECHNIQUE

Shake the milk, tea concentrate, rum, cardamom, salt, and pepper with ice for several seconds, until chilled. Strain into a lowball glass with 1 large ice cube. Garnish with the star anise.

THE MILKY MOON.

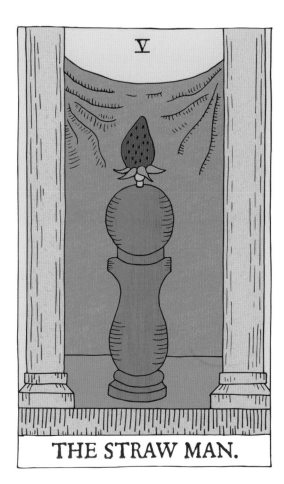

THE STRAW MAN.

THE STRAW MAN

Sweet strawberries get a dose of depth thanks to black pepper and balsamic vinegar. As you enjoy, let go of something masquerading as important.

INGREDIENTS

2 to 3 fresh strawberries
1½ ounces vodka
½ ounce Black Pepper Syrup (see below)
½ teaspoon balsamic vinegar
2 ounces soda water

Garnish
Strawberry

TECHNIQUE

Hull and slice the strawberries into your shaker and then muddle them. Add the vodka, syrup, and balsamic vinegar, and shake with ice for several seconds, until chilled. Double strain through a Hawthorne strainer and fine-mesh sieve into a highball glass filled with ice. Top with the soda and gently stir. Garnish with the strawberry.

BLACK PEPPER SYRUP

Makes about 1½ cups

Heat 1 cup water, 1 cup sugar, and 1 teaspoon freshly ground black pepper in a saucepan over medium heat, stirring until the sugar has dissolved completely. Let cool and stir or shake before each use. Keep refrigerated in a covered container for up to 1 month.

THE GRAIL

In the fruity, full-bodied Grail, fig butter and muddled cherries combine with syrah to create a jammy but not-too-sweet profile, while bourbon adds a boozy kick. As you enjoy, follow the gently tugging thread of your intuition to find what you need.

Tip: Skip the neon-red cherries and spring for the good ones—they're worth it.

INGREDIENTS

3 quality maraschino cherries
1 teaspoon fig butter
1 ounce bourbon
1½ ounces syrah
2 dashes of Angostura bitters

Garnish
Maraschino cherries

TECHNIQUE

Muddle the cherries in your shaker. Add the fig butter, bourbon, syrah, and bitters and shake with ice for several seconds, until chilled. Strain through a fine-mesh sieve into a chilled coupe glass. Garnish with the maraschino cherries.

VI

THE GRAIL.

VII

QUEEN ⚜ BEES.

QUEEN OF BEES

Inspired by the classic Bee's Knees cocktail (simply gin, lemon, and honey), Queen of Bees includes sparkling wine for a bit of spritz and lavender water, which lends a light, floral essence. As you enjoy, pollinate the people around you with positivity.

INGREDIENTS

1 ounce dry gin
½ ounce Honey Syrup (see below)
½ ounce freshly squeezed lemon juice
5 dashes of lavender water
2 ounces dry sparkling wine

Garnish
Lemon wheel

TECHNIQUE

Shake the gin, syrup, juice, and lavender water with ice for several seconds, until chilled. Strain into a lowball glass filled with ice. Top with the sparkling wine and gently stir. Garnish with the lemon wheel.

HONEY SYRUP

Combine equal parts honey and water in a saucepan over medium heat, stirring until the honey has dissolved completely. Let cool before using. Keep refrigerated in a covered container for up to 2 weeks.

SPICE OF LIFE

Invigorate your senses with this spicy kick of a cocktail. As you enjoy, appreciate the stunning array of variety that surrounds you.

INGREDIENTS

1½ ounces reposado tequila
½ ounce freshly squeezed lemon juice
½ ounce Ginger-Chili Syrup (see below)
2 ounces soda water

Garnish
Slapped basil leaves

TECHNIQUE

Shake the tequila, juice, and syrup with ice for several seconds, until chilled. Strain into a highball glass filled with ice. Top with soda and gently stir. Garnish with the slapped basil.

GINGER-CHILI SYRUP

Makes about 1 cup

Combine 1 cup sugar, 1 cup water, ½ cup grated fresh ginger, and ½ teaspoon red chili flakes in a saucepan over medium heat. Simmer for 10 to 15 minutes, stirring often. Let cool and strain. Keep refrigerated in a covered container for up to 1 month.

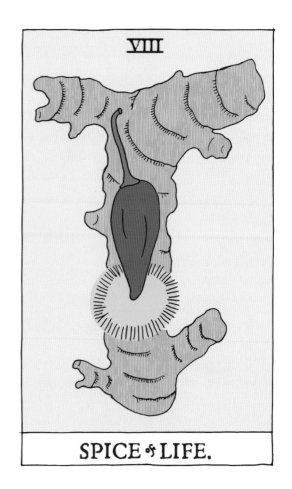

VIII

SPICE ⚜ LIFE.

PITH OF STICKS.

PITH OF STICKS

In the mood for a summery cocktail in the dead of winter? Look no further than this season-defying drink. Bittersweet grapefruit and spicy cinnamon make for a delightfully bright combination in Pith of Sticks. As you enjoy, peel back the layers to get at the heart of something.

INGREDIENTS

2 ounces freshly squeezed grapefruit juice
1½ ounces light rum
½ ounce Cinnamon Syrup (see below)
½ ounce freshly squeezed lime juice
3 dashes of Angostura bitters

Garnish
Grapefruit wedge

TECHNIQUE

Shake the grapefruit juice, rum, syrup, and lime juice with ice for several seconds, until chilled. Strain into a chilled coupe glass and top with the bitters. Garnish with the grapefruit wedge.

CINNAMON SYRUP

Makes about 1½ cups

Combine 1 cup sugar, 1 cup water, and 1 teaspoon cinnamon in a saucepan over medium heat, stirring until the sugar has dissolved completely. Let cool before using. Keep refrigerated in a covered container for up to 1 month.

PRINCESS OF MOSCOW

Based on the Moscow Mule, this fancy float boasts spicy ginger, ice-cold vodka, and a double dose of lime. As you enjoy, know that you deserve a decadent indulgence.

INGREDIENTS

3 ounces chilled ginger beer
1½ ounces chilled vodka
¼ ounce freshly squeezed lime juice
1 scoop lime sherbet

Garnish
Lime wedge and candied ginger

TECHNIQUE

Combine the ginger beer, vodka, and juice in a lowball glass and gently stir. Then add the sherbet. Garnish with the lime wedge and candied ginger.

PRINCESS ⚜ MOSCOW.

THE ARCHER.

THE ARCHER

Herbaceous and tart with a touch of sweetness, The Archer is a zingy sipper with the quality of a shrub, also known as a drinking vinegar. As you enjoy, set your sights and watch your intentions sail toward the target.

INGREDIENTS

1½ ounces dry gin
½ ounce freshly squeezed lemon juice
½ ounce Rosemary Syrup (see below)
¼ teaspoon apple cider vinegar

Garnish
Rosemary sprig

TECHNIQUE

Shake the gin, juice, syrup, and vinegar with ice for several seconds, until chilled. Strain into a chilled coupe glass and garnish with the rosemary sprig.

ROSEMARY SYRUP

Makes about 1 cup

Combine 1 cup sugar, 1 cup water, and 4 rosemary sprigs in a saucepan over medium heat. Simmer for 10 to 15 minutes, stirring until the sugar has dissolved. Let cool and strain before using. Discard the rosemary sprigs. Keep refrigerated in a covered container for up to 1 month.

THE FEAST

Inspired by the fruits and spices of Thanksgiving, The Feast will summon a celebratory spirit. Zesty orange, tart cranberry, warming cinnamon, rich brown sugar, and dry rye whiskey come together to create a cornucopia of flavor. As you enjoy, meditate on good fortune and gratitude.

INGREDIENTS

1½ ounces rye whiskey
1 ounce 100 percent cranberry juice
½ ounce Cinnamon–Brown Sugar Syrup (see below)
2 ounces soda water
2 dashes of orange bitters

Garnish
Orange wedge, cranberries, and cinnamon stick

TECHNIQUE

Shake the whiskey, juice, and syrup with ice for several seconds, until chilled. Strain into a lowball glass filled with ice. Top with the soda and bitters and gently stir. Garnish with the orange wedge, cranberries, and cinnamon stick.

CINNAMON–BROWN SUGAR SYRUP

Makes about 1½ cups

Combine 1 cup brown sugar, 1 cup water, and 1 teaspoon ground cinnamon over medium heat, stirring until the sugar has dissolved completely. Remove from the heat and let cool before using. Keep refrigerated in a covered container for up to 1 month.

THE FEAST.

XIII

ROOT ᕯ ALL.

ROOT OF ALL

Striking the perfect balance of bitter and sweet, Root of All is a robust, boozy blend. Don't be fooled by the root beer—this cocktail is all grown up, thanks in part to the complexity imparted by Cynar, an Italian amaro, or bitter liqueur. Served over a large ice cube, it's meant to be sipped, so you can savor every flavor. As you enjoy, marvel at the origin of something important.

INGREDIENTS

1½ ounces reposado tequila

½ ounce Cynar

2 ounces chilled root beer

2 dashes of Angostura bitters

TECHNIQUE

Stir the tequila and Cynar with ice until chilled. Strain into a lowball glass with 1 large ice cube. Add the root beer and gently stir. Top with the bitters.

THE FIRST MAN

Rich, creamy coconut; sweet and tart apricot; exotic allspice dram; and gold rum come together to create a tropical tiki vibe. As you enjoy, appreciate the expanse of experience and your special place in it.

Tip: Allspice dram, also known as pimento dram, can be found at most liquor stores. None on hand? You can use Cinnamon Syrup (page 19) as a substitute.

INGREDIENTS

2 ounces apricot nectar
1½ ounces gold rum
1½ ounces unsweetened coconut cream
½ ounce allspice dram

Garnish
Ground cinnamon and a cocktail umbrella

TECHNIQUE

Blend the nectar, rum, coconut cream, and allspice dram in a blender until smooth. Shake the blended mixture with ice for several seconds, until chilled. Strain into a coconut cup or tiki mug filled with ice. Garnish with a sprinkle of cinnamon and the cocktail umbrella.

THE FIRST MAN.

THE ELDER.

THE ELDER

A wise choice indeed. The combination of gin, lemon, and elderflower is delicately delicious. But The Elder's hint of sherry, a Spanish fortified wine, takes it to the next level. Light-bodied without being boring, it's a truly lovely libation. As you enjoy, raise your glass to the sage in your life.

Tip: You can find elderflower syrup at most liquor stores, specialty grocery stores, and even IKEA.

INGREDIENTS

1½ ounces dry gin
½ ounce elderflower syrup
¼ ounce amontillado sherry
¼ ounce freshly squeezed lemon juice
2 ounces soda water

Garnish
Lemon wheel

TECHNIQUE

Shake the gin, syrup, sherry, and juice with ice for several seconds, until chilled. Strain into a highball glass filled with ice. Top with the soda and gently stir. Garnish with the lemon wheel.

THE TRIPLE CROWN

Based on the classic mint julep, The Triple Crown blends rich brown sugar, aromatic mint, effervescent sparkling wine, and plenty of bourbon to arrive at a winning cocktail. As you enjoy, take a moment to jubilate your journey.

INGREDIENTS

10 mint leaves
½ ounce Brown Sugar Syrup (see below)
2 ounces bourbon
3 ounces dry sparkling wine

Garnish
Mint sprig

TECHNIQUE

Gently muddle the mint and syrup in a julep cup. Fill the cup with crushed ice, add the bourbon, and gently stir. Top with the sparkling wine. Garnish with the mint sprig.

BROWN SUGAR SYRUP

Combine equal parts brown sugar and water in a saucepan over medium heat, stirring until the sugar has dissolved completely. Remove from the heat and let cool before using. Keep refrigerated in a covered container for up to 1 month.

THE TRIPLE CROWN.

XVII

ARC of TIME.

ARC OF TIME

Juicy blackberries, herbaceous thyme, and reposado tequila harmonize into an earthy base. Exotic falernum (a liqueur often used in Caribbean drinks) adds some sugar and spice. Lime and soda keep things light and fresh. As you enjoy, acknowledge how yesterday and tomorrow dance with today.

Tip: You can find falernum at most liquor stores. None on hand? You can leave it out and replace the soda with 3 ounces of ginger beer for an equally delicious drink.

INGREDIENTS

Several sprigs of thyme
¼ cup blackberries
1½ ounces reposado tequila
1 ounce falernum
¼ ounce freshly squeezed lime juice
2 dashes of Angostura bitters
2 ounces soda water

Garnish
Slapped thyme and blackberries

TECHNIQUE

Place the thyme in your shaker, then add the blackberries and muddle. Add the tequila, falernum, juice, and bitters, and shake with ice for several seconds, until chilled. Double strain through a Hawthorne strainer and fine-mesh sieve into a highball glass filled with ice. Top with the soda and gently stir. Garnish with the slapped thyme and a few blackberries.

BREAK OF DAWN

While the beloved Bloody Mary is already bursting with flavor, Break of Dawn throws in a few more for good measure. Earthy beets, sweet carrots, and spicy ginger make for a slightly lighter Bloody with fresh-from-the-garden taste. As you enjoy, delight in some downtime, and share a sip with the sun.

INGREDIENTS

Coarse salt and freshly ground black pepper, for rim

2 ounces tomato juice

1½ ounces vodka

1 ounce beet juice

½ ounce carrot juice

2 dashes of hot sauce

¼ ounce freshly squeezed lemon juice

¼ teaspoon ground ginger

Garnish

Pickled beets

TECHNIQUE

Rim a highball glass with a mixture of coarse salt and ground black pepper (3 parts salt to 1 part pepper). Shake the tomato juice, vodka, beet juice, carrot juice, hot sauce, lemon juice, and ground ginger with ice for several seconds, until chilled. Strain into the rimmed highball glass filled with ice. Garnish with the pickled beets.

BREAK ⚜ DAWN.

THE CLIMBING VINE

A twist on the classic martini, The Climbing Vine swaps amontillado sherry for vermouth and opts for orange bitters in lieu of olives. The result is dry and botanical with a hint of bright citrus. As you enjoy, ponder your potential for growth.

INGREDIENTS

2½ ounces dry gin
¾ ounce amontillado sherry
3 dashes of orange bitters

Garnish

Orange twist

TECHNIQUE

Stir the gin and sherry with ice until chilled. Strain into a chilled coupe glass and top with the bitters. Garnish with the orange twist.

THE WHITE ELEPHANT

The original daiquiri (simply rum, sugar, and lime) got a bit of a bad reputation thanks to artificial strawberry abominations, but this classic has made a comeback. The White Elephant takes the Hemingway Daiquiri (which features the addition of grapefruit juice and maraschino liqueur) and adds another twist in the form of egg white. The light, fruity, frothy result is like a cloud in cocktail form . . . with enough rum to pack a punch. As you enjoy, engage your imagination, and find magic in the mundane.

INGREDIENTS

2 ounces white rum

¾ ounce freshly squeezed grapefruit juice

1 egg white

½ ounce freshly squeezed lime juice

¼ ounce maraschino liqueur

¼ ounce Simple Syrup (page xi)

Garnish

Maraschino cherry

TECHNIQUE

Dry shake (without ice) the rum, grapefruit juice, egg white, lime juice, liqueur, and syrup for about 15 seconds. Add ice and shake again for several seconds, until chilled. Strain into a chilled coupe glass. Garnish with the maraschino cherry.

THE WHITE ELEPHANT.

THE BLACK NIGHT.

THE BLACK NIGHT

Reminiscent of a cherry cola but with the added indulgence of chocolate and bourbon, The Black Night has dessert-like qualities without being heavy. The hint of balsamic is not a primary flavor but serves to enhance the overall profile. This dark, rich drink is the perfect candidate if you're in the mood for a not-too-sweet treat. As you enjoy, let out a cathartic howl at the moon.

Tip: Maraschino syrup (dark and thick) is not to be confused with maraschino liqueur (clear and thin). You can buy the syrup bottled or use the liquid from your jar of cherries.

INGREDIENTS

1½ ounces bourbon
¾ ounce maraschino syrup
1 teaspoon balsamic vinegar
4 ounces chocolate stout

Garnish
Maraschino cherries

TECHNIQUE

Shake the bourbon, syrup, and vinegar with ice for several seconds, until chilled. Strain into a highball glass filled with ice. Top with the chocolate stout and gently stir. Garnish with a few maraschino cherries.

THE VIOLET TWILIGHT

Inspired by the classic Negroni (gin, Campari, and sweet vermouth), The Violet Twilight is distinctly bitter and sweet with a subtle floral note and beautiful deep color. If a light, goes-down-easy drink is the bright sun, and a strong, spirit-forward sipper is the dark night, think of this cocktail as that magical half-light. As you enjoy, appreciate the nuance of in-betweens.

Tip: Violet liqueur, also known as crème de violette, can be found at most liquor stores.

INGREDIENTS

1 ounce dry gin
1 ounce dry vermouth
½ ounce Campari
½ ounce violet liqueur

Garnish
Orange twist

TECHNIQUE

Shake the gin, vermouth, Campari, and violet liqueur with ice for several seconds, until chilled. Strain into a chilled coupe glass. Garnish with the orange twist.

THE VIOLET TWILIGHT.

THE SUNDIAL.

THE SUNDIAL

The Sundial, a refreshing frozen margarita variation with hints of heat and sweet, is ideal for island escapes—both real and imaginary. As you enjoy, allow yourself to lose track of time.

INGREDIENTS

Salt, sugar, and cayenne, for rim
1½ ounces reposado tequila
1½ ounces unsweetened coconut milk
1 ounce triple sec
1 ounce freshly squeezed lime juice
½ cup frozen mango chunks
½ cup cubed ice
2 slices fresh jalapeño, seeds removed

Garnish
Lime wheel

TECHNIQUE

Rim a lowball glass with a mixture of equal parts salt and sugar, plus a pinch of cayenne. Blend the tequila, coconut milk, triple sec, juice, mango, ice, and jalapeño slices in a blender until smooth. Pour into the rimmed glass. Garnish with the lime wheel.

WINTER'S PEAK

What could be merrier than a mash-up of the two most beloved drinks of the holiday season? Winter's Peak brings together creamy eggnog and rich, spicy Mexican hot chocolate for a festive confection that will warm you from the inside. As you enjoy, envelop yourself in the kindness of the season.

INGREDIENTS

6 ounces premade eggnog
1½ ounces bourbon
1 teaspoon cocoa powder
¼ teaspoon cinnamon
1 small pinch of cayenne

Garnish
Nutmeg, cocoa powder, and a cinnamon stick

TECHNIQUE

Combine the eggnog, bourbon, cocoa, cinnamon, and cayenne in a saucepan over low heat, stirring until it's well-mixed and warm. Remove from the heat, pour into a mug, and sprinkle with nutmeg and cocoa powder. Garnish with the cinnamon stick.

WINTER'S PEAK.

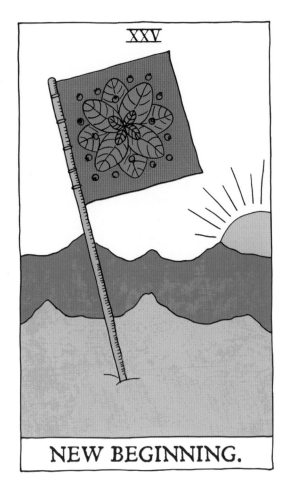

NEW BEGINNING

Start fresh with this vibrant cocktail. Verdant basil, juicy blueberries, and botanical gin create a full-flavored yet mellow medley. As you enjoy, consider an exhilarating change.

Small handful of basil leaves
¼ cup blueberries
1½ ounces dry gin
½ ounce Simple Syrup (page xi)
¼ ounce freshly squeezed lemon juice
2 ounces soda water

Garnish
Basil and blueberries

TECHNIQUE
Muddle the basil and blueberries in your shaker. Add the gin, syrup, and juice, then shake with ice for several seconds, until chilled. Double strain through a Hawthorne strainer and fine-mesh sieve into a lowball glass filled with ice. Top with the soda and gently stir. Garnish with basil leaves and a few blueberries.

THE GOLD STANDARD

Salted honey syrup makes the apricot, lemon, and rye truly shine in the refreshing Gold Standard. Like liquid sunshine, this enchanting elixir is worth its weight in gold. As you enjoy, remember you have value beyond measure.

INGREDIENTS

1½ ounces rye whiskey
1 ounce apricot nectar
½ ounce freshly squeezed lemon juice
½ ounce Salted Honey Syrup (see below)
2 ounces soda water

Garnish
Lemon wedge

TECHNIQUE

Shake the whiskey, nectar, juice, and syrup with ice for several seconds, until chilled. Strain into a highball glass filled with ice. Top with the soda and gently stir. Garnish with the lemon wedge.

SALTED HONEY SYRUP

Makes about 2 cups

Combine 1 cup honey, 1 cup water, and 1 teaspoon salt in a saucepan over medium heat, stirring until the honey and salt have dissolved completely. Remove from heat and let cool before using. Keep refrigerated in a covered container for up to 2 weeks.

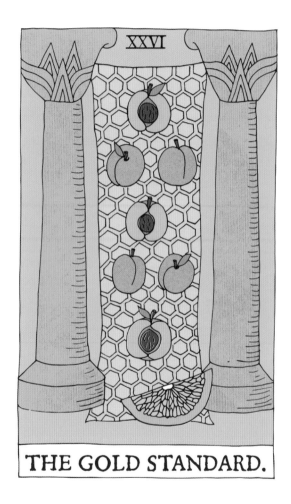

THE GOLD STANDARD.

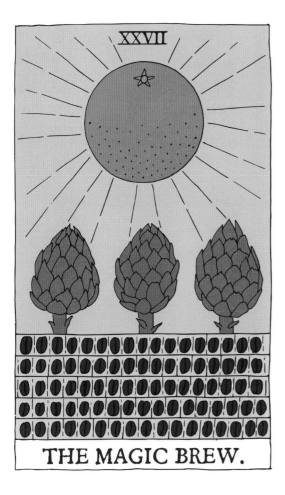

THE MAGIC BREW

Fire burn and cauldron bubble—you toil hard, so make it a double. The bold Magic Brew brings your morning muse to cocktail hour. This dynamic drink marries the rich, dark goodness of coffee with bittersweet Cynar (an Italian amaro), vibrant orange liqueur, and full-bodied bourbon. As you enjoy, cast a spell of calmness, and allow the grind of the day to fall away.

INGREDIENTS

1½ ounces bourbon
1 ounce cold strong coffee
½ ounce Cynar
½ ounce triple sec

Garnish
Orange twist

TECHNIQUE

Shake the bourbon, coffee, Cynar, and triple sec with ice for several seconds, until chilled. Strain into a lowball glass with 1 large ice cube. Garnish with the orange twist.

FLOWER OF PALMS

The creamy coconut and fresh citrus in Flower of Palms recall Brazilian lemonade, while the rose water and cinnamon evoke ambrosial desserts like baklava. As you enjoy, appreciate the beauty that blossoms from your hardworking hands.

INGREDIENTS

2 ounces water
1½ ounces light rum
1 ounce unsweetened coconut cream
1 ounce freshly squeezed lemon juice
1 ounce Cinnamon Syrup (page 19)
½ teaspoon rose water

Garnish
Edible rose petals and cinnamon

TECHNIQUE

Blend the water, rum, coconut cream, juice, syrup, and rose water in a blender without ice until smooth. Shake the blended mixture with ice for several seconds, until chilled. Strain into a lowball glass filled with ice. Garnish with the rose petals and a sprinkle of cinnamon.

XXVIII

FLOWER ⚜ PALMS.

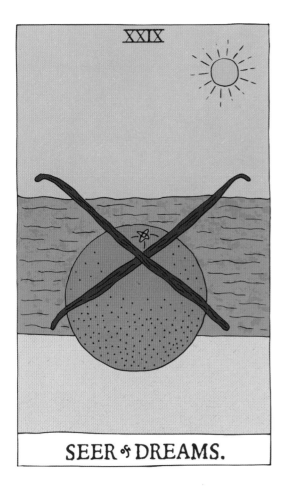

SEER OF DREAMS

With its soda pop of color, Seer of Dreams is a bright, carefree float. Smooth vanilla ice cream and tangy orange offer up a sweet taste of summers past, while the bourbon adds a rich new dimension. As you enjoy, allow yourself to revel in nostalgia.

INGREDIENTS

4 ounces chilled orange soda
1½ ounces bourbon
1 scoop vanilla ice cream

Garnish
Orange wedge

TECHNIQUE

Combine the soda and bourbon in a lowball glass and stir. Add the ice cream. Garnish with the orange wedge.

THE BITTER TRUTH

Campari is a bitter liqueur, grapefruit is a bitter fruit, and IPA contains bitter hops. Notice a pattern? A dainty dose of sweetness balances the scale, but if you're not keen on bitterness, this might not be your cup o' booze. If bitter is your favored flavor, get to mixing this low-proof libation. As you enjoy, remember to take the bitter with the sweet—happiness hangs in the balance.

INGREDIENTS

1 ounce freshly squeezed grapefruit juice
½ ounce Campari
¼ ounce Simple Syrup (page xi)
3 ounces IPA

Garnish
Grapefruit twist

TECHNIQUE

Shake the juice, Campari, and syrup with ice for several seconds, until chilled. Strain into a highball glass filled with ice. Top with the IPA and gently stir. Garnish with a grapefruit twist.

THE BITTER TRUTH.

XXXI

NECTAR of the GODS.

NECTAR OF THE GODS

Inspired by the flavors of baklava, Nectar of the Gods is a trifle dessert-like while staying shy of saccharine. Rum and honey create a toothsome treat, while the lemon brings balance. A rose water rinse adds a barely there essence of floral, and the egg white lends luscious texture. As you enjoy, remember to savor the sips of sweetness in this life.

INGREDIENTS

Rose water, for rinsing glass
2 ounces aged gold rum
1 ounce Honey Syrup (page 15)
½ ounce freshly squeezed lemon juice
1 egg white

Garnish
Ground cardamom and crushed pistachios

TECHNIQUE

Pour a small amount of rose water into a coupe glass, twirl to coat, and dump any that remains. Dry shake (without ice) the rum, syrup, juice, and egg white for 15 seconds. Add ice and shake again for several seconds, until chilled. Strain into your rinsed glass and top with a sprinkle of cardamom and a few crushed pistachios.

THE BELL TOWER

Vegetal yellow pepper and stimulating mint complement earthy Scotch, while pineapple provides some tropical zest in the fresh, multifaceted Bell Tower. As you enjoy, listen for a signal that might be calling to you.

Tip: Fresh fruit and vegetable juices are all the rage these days, and most grocery stores carry a good selection. Find a premade juice with similar ingredients to those in this recipe to bypass the process of juicing your own produce.

INGREDIENTS

Small handful of mint leaves
1½ ounces smoky Scotch
1 ounce yellow bell pepper juice
1 ounce fresh pineapple juice
¼ ounce Simple Syrup (page xi)
¼ ounce freshly squeezed lime juice

Garnish
Mint leaves

TECHNIQUE

Gently muddle the mint leaves in your shaker. Add the Scotch, bell pepper juice, pineapple juice, syrup, and lime juice and shake with ice for several seconds, until chilled. Strain into a highball glass filled with ice. Garnish with a bouquet of mint leaves.

XXXII

THE BELL TOWER.

THE FIRST BLUSH.

THE FIRST BLUSH

Tangy-meets-sweet rhubarb syrup, honeyed floral Lillet, and crisp gin make friends with refreshing rosé in this pretty pink drink. As you enjoy, fall in love at first sight, if only for a moment.

INGREDIENTS

3 ounces rosé wine
1 ounce dry gin
1 ounce Lillet
½ ounce Rhubarb Syrup (see below)

Garnish
Raspberries

TECHNIQUE

Shake the wine, gin, Lillet, and syrup with ice for several seconds, until chilled. Strain into a highball glass filled with ice. Garnish with a few floating raspberries.

RHUBARB SYRUP

Makes about 1½ cups

Combine 1 cup water, 1 cup sugar, and 2 cups chopped rhubarb in a saucepan over medium heat. Bring to a boil. Lower the heat and simmer for 10 to 15 minutes. Remove from the heat, let cool completely, and strain through a fine-mesh sieve. Discard the rhubarb pieces. Keep the syrup refrigerated in a covered container for up to 1 month.

MONK OF THE MOUNTAINS

Infused with more than a hundred herbs, Chartreuse is a French liqueur that has been produced by Carthusian monks for centuries. This sweet yet deep drink warms the palate with just a few ingredients, including yellow Chartreuse, the mellower brother of the well-known green variety. The flavors come through strong and true, without distraction. As you enjoy, clear your mind and allow the fluff to fall away.

INGREDIENTS

1½ ounces bourbon
½ ounce yellow Chartreuse
½ ounce sweet vermouth
2 dashes of Angostura bitters

Garnish
Lemon twist

TECHNIQUE

Stir the bourbon, Chartreuse, and vermouth with ice until chilled. Strain into a lowball glass over a big cube. Top with the bitters and garnish with the lemon twist.

MONK of the MOUNTAINS.

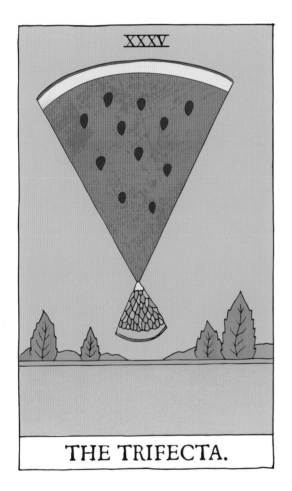

XXXV

THE TRIFECTA.

THE TRIFECTA

Summery watermelon, invigorating mint, and tangy lime coalesce to form a tasty triptych. This carefree cocktail is magical on a muggy day. As you enjoy, let yourself lag to a languid pace for a little while.

INGREDIENTS

Small handful of mint
½ cup cubed watermelon
1½ ounces light rum
¼ ounce Simple Syrup (page xi)
¼ ounce freshly squeezed lime juice
Pinch of salt

Garnish
Lime wheel

TECHNIQUE

Place the mint in the bottom of your shaker, then add the watermelon and muddle until all the large chunks are eliminated. Add the rum, syrup, juice, and salt, and shake with ice for several seconds, until chilled. Double strain through a Hawthorne strainer and fine-mesh sieve into a highball glass filled with ice. Garnish with the lime wheel.

THE MIRAGE

Although it takes notes from the Negroni, this spirit-forward sipper paints a vision all its own. Sweet, bitter, and boozy flavors dance fancifully on the palate. As you enjoy, visualize a moment you'd like to manifest.

INGREDIENTS

1½ ounces reposado tequila

¾ ounce Aperol

¾ ounce sweet vermouth

Garnish

Orange twist (optional)

TECHNIQUE

Stir the tequila, Aperol, and sweet vermouth with ice until chilled. Strain into a lowball glass over a big cube. Garnish with the orange twist.

THE FLOWER CROWN

The classic, soothing combination of earthy chamomile, delicate honey, and zesty lemon is chained together with smoky Scotch and herbal Chartreuse to complete the circle of this pleasing drink. As you enjoy, play a little game of *"I love me . . . I love me lots."*

INGREDIENTS

2 ounces strong chamomile tea, cooled

1½ ounces Scotch

½ ounce yellow Chartreuse

¼ ounce Honey Syrup (page 15)

¼ ounce freshly squeezed lemon juice

TECHNIQUE

Shake the tea, Scotch, Chartreuse, syrup, and juice with ice for several seconds, until chilled. Strain into a lowball glass filled with ice.

THE CALYPSO

The working title of this drink was "A Rum and Coke That's Actually Good." There's nothing wrong with enjoying the popular pairing, but you won't find many cocktail connoisseurs singing its praises. This version benefits from a not-too-sweet balance of cola and spirits, the richness of aged rum, the aromatic bitterness of Fernet, and just a hint of chocolate. As you enjoy, reimagine the mundane.

INGREDIENTS

4 ounces chilled cola

1½ ounces aged añejo rum

¼ ounce Fernet

5 dashes of chocolate bitters

TECHNIQUE

Combine the cola, rum, and Fernet in a lowball glass filled with ice and gently stir. Top with the bitters.

XXXVIII

THE CALYPSO.

THE ROSE-COLORED GLASS.

THE ROSE-COLORED GLASS

Play up the positivity with this charming treat. Fresh raspberries and lemon curd lend lively sweet and sour notes, while gin and Campari keep things complex. As you enjoy, optimize your outlook with a lens of love.

INGREDIENTS

¼ cup raspberries
1½ ounces dry gin
¼ ounce Campari
¼ ounce Simple Syrup (page xi)
1 teaspoon lemon curd
2 ounces soda water

Garnish
Raspberries

TECHNIQUE

Muddle the raspberries in your shaker. Add the gin, Campari, syrup, and lemon curd, and shake with ice for several seconds, until chilled. Double strain through a Hawthorne strainer and fine-mesh sieve into a highball glass filled with ice. Top with the soda and gently stir. Garnish with a few raspberries.

SWEET SURRENDER

Allow yourself a little escape with a Sweet Surrender. Based on Vietnamese iced coffee, this buzzy beverage boasts bold coffee flavor, creamy sweetness, and a bit of bite. As you enjoy, perk up your perspective, pay attention to the details around you, and just exist in the moment.

INGREDIENTS

2 ounces cold strong coffee
1 ounce bourbon
1 ounce sweetened condensed milk
¼ ounce Fernet

TECHNIQUE

Shake the coffee, bourbon, condensed milk, and Fernet with ice for several seconds, until chilled. Strain into a highball glass filled with ice.

SWEET SURRENDER.

CITY OF EMERALD.

CITY OF EMERALD

Go green with some fresh, grassy goodness. Sharp and tart yet earthy and herbaceous, this juicy jade-colored concoction doesn't shy away from flavor. As you enjoy, revel in the resplendence of your own realm.

Tip: If you don't have a juicer, blend chopped celery and apples in a blender until smooth, then strain through a fine-mesh sieve or a nut milk bag.

INGREDIENTS

Celery salt, for rim (optional)
1½ ounces blanco tequila
1 ounce celery juice
1 ounce Granny Smith apple juice
½ ounce freshly squeezed lime juice
½ ounce green Chartreuse

Garnish
Celery ribbon

TECHNIQUE

If desired, rim a chilled coupe glass with celery salt and set aside. Shake the tequila, celery juice, apple juice, lime juice, and Chartreuse with ice for several seconds, until chilled. Strain into your glass and garnish with the celery ribbon.

THE POINTED LEAF

There's something so singular about autumn, and this cocktail captures a little taste of that magic. Imagine brisk morning air, trees afire with warm orange hues, and the spiced scent of pipe smoke. With its rich, rounded flavor profile, the spirit-forward Pointed Leaf will fill you with that fall feeling. As you enjoy, hunker down in hibernation for an evening.

INGREDIENTS

1 ounce apple brandy
½ ounce Scotch
¼ ounce medium sherry
2 teaspoons maple syrup
3 dashes of walnut bitters

TECHNIQUE

Shake the brandy, Scotch, sherry, and syrup with ice for several seconds, until chilled. Strain into a lowball glass over a big cube and top with the bitters.

THE POINTED LEAF.

XLIII

MILK of GOLD.

MILK OF GOLD

Bolstered by the anti-inflammatory qualities of turmeric, Golden Milk has made a mighty mark in the world of holistic wellness. Health claims aside, your senses will benefit from the stunning sunshine yellow and spicy bite of this honey-sweetened mixture. As you enjoy, consider the golden riches in your land of milk and honey.

INGREDIENTS

1½ ounces aged gold rum
4 ounces unsweetened coconut milk
½ teaspoon ground turmeric
½ teaspoon ground ginger
½ ounce honey

TECHNIQUE

Combine the rum, coconut milk, turmeric, ginger, and honey in a saucepan over medium heat, stirring until the ingredients are well-blended and the mixture is hot. Remove from heat and pour into a mug to enjoy warm, or let cool and pour through a fine-mesh sieve into a glass filled with ice.

THE HEDGE MAZE

The flavor of this dynamic, layered drink is hard to ascertain . . . in the most exciting way. Find your way through smoky notes, citrus peel, a bit of bitter, and fragrant fresh herbs. As you enjoy, ponder a perplexing puzzle.

INGREDIENTS

Coarse salt, for rimming glass
1 small handful of fresh cilantro
¼ ounce Simple Syrup (page xi)
1 ounce mezcal
½ ounce tequila
¼ ounce curaçao
¼ ounce Cynar
¼ ounce freshly squeezed lime juice

Garnish
Slapped cilantro

TECHNIQUE

Rim a chilled coupe glass with salt. Gently muddle the cilantro and syrup in your shaker. Add the mezcal, tequila, curaçao, Cynar, and lime juice and shake with ice for several seconds, until chilled. Strain through a fine-mesh sieve into your rimmed glass. Garnish with a few sprigs of slapped cilantro.

XLIV

THE HEDGE MAZE.

THE LAMB'S TAIL.

THE LAMB'S TAIL

Part milkshake, part fruit smoothie, part cocktail, this rich, sweet amalgamation has many appetizing facets. As you enjoy, don't feel like you have to rush to the next thing— be soft on yourself.

INGREDIENTS

4 ounces milk (or milk alternative)
1½ ounces añejo rum
1 frozen chopped banana
1 teaspoon cocoa powder

TECHNIQUE

Blend the milk, rum, banana, and cocoa in a blender until smooth. Serve in a highball glass with a paper or metal straw.

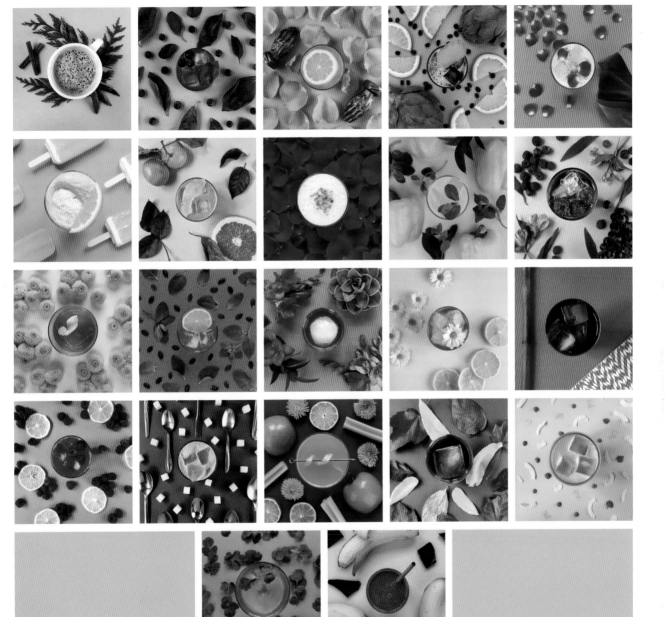

INDEX

A

allspice dram, 28–29
amontillado sherry, 30–31, 38–39
Angostura bitters, 12–13, 18–19, 26–27, 34–35, 68–69
Aperol, 72–73
apple brandy, 84–85
apple cider vinegar, 22–23
apple juice, 82–83
apricot nectar, 28–29, 52–53

B

balsamic vinegar, 10–11, 42–43
banana, 90–91
barspoon, x
basil, 16–17, 50–51
beer, 4–5, 42–43, 60–61
beets/beet juice, 36–37
bell pepper, yellow, 64–65
black pepper, 8–9, 36–37
   Black Pepper Syrup, 10–11
blackberries, 34–35
blood orange, 2–3
blueberries, 50–51
bourbon
   The Black Night, 42–43
   The Grail, 12–13
   The Magic Brew, 54–55
   Monk of the Mountains, 68–69
   Rule of Three, 6–7
   Seer of Dreams, 58–59
   Sweet Surrender, 80–81
   The Triple Crown, 32–33
   Winter's Peak, 48–49
brown sugar
   Brown Sugar Syrup, 32–33
   Cinnamon–Brown Sugar Syrup, 24–25

C

Campari
   The Bitter Truth, 60–61
   The Rose-Colored Glass, 78–79

   The Violet Twilight, 44–45
cardamom, 8–9, 62–63
carrot juice, 36–37
cayenne, 48–49
celery/celery juice, 82–83
chai tea, 8–9
chamomile tea, 74–75
Chartreuse, green, 82–83
Chartreuse, yellow, 68–69, 74–75
chili flakes, 16–17
chocolate bitters, 76–77
chocolate stout, 42–43
cilantro, 88–89
cinnamon, 48–49
   Cinnamon Syrup, 18–19, 56–57
   Cinnamon–Brown Sugar Syrup, 24–25
citrus twist, creating, xiv
cocoa powder
   The Lamb's Tail, 90–91
   Winter's Peak, 48–49
coconut milk/cream
   The First Man, 28–29
   Flower of Palms, 56–57
   Milk of Gold, 86–87
   The Sundial, 46–47
coffee
   The Magic Brew, 54–55
   Sweet Surrender, 80–81
cola, 76–77
condensed milk, 80–81
cranberry juice, 24–25
Cynar
   The Hedge Maze, 88–89
   The Magic Brew, 54–55
   Root of All, 26–27

E

egg whites, xiv, 40–41, 62–63
eggnog, 48–49
elderflower syrup, 30–31

F

falernum, 34–35
Fernet, 76–77, 80–81
fig butter, 12–13

G

garnishes, about, xiii, xiv
gin, dry
   The Archer, 22–23
   The Climbing Vine, 38–39
   The Elder, 30–31
   The First Blush, 66–67
   The Herbalist, 4–5
   New Beginning, 50–51
   Queen of Bees, 14–15
   The Rose-Colored Glass, 78–79
   The Violet Twilight, 44–45
ginger
   Break of Dawn, 36–37
   Ginger-Chili Syrup, 16–17
   Milk of Gold, 86–87
ginger beer, 20–21
glassware, xi
grapefruit/grapefruit juice, 18–19, 40–41, 60–61

H

herbs, slapped, xiv
honey, 86–87
   Honey Syrup, 14–15
   Salted Honey Syrup, 52–53, 62–63, 74–75
hot sauce, 36–37

I

ice, about, xii
ingredients, xii–xv
IPA, 4–5, 60–61

J

jalapeño, 46–47
jigger, ix

L

lavender water, 14–15
lemon curd, 78–79
lemons/lemon juice, 6–7, 14–15, 16–17,
    22–23, 30–31, 36–37, 50–51, 52–53,
    56–57, 68–69, 74–75
Lillet, 66–67
lime sherbet, 20–21
limes/lime juice, 18–19, 20–21, 34–35,
    40–41, 46–47, 64–65, 70–71, 82–83,
    88–89
liqueurs, about, xiii

M

mango, 46–47
maple syrup, 84–85
maraschino cherries, 12–13, 40–41,
    42–43
maraschino liqueur, 2–3, 40–41
maraschino syrup, 42–43
measurements, ix
mezcal
    Blood and Smoke, 2–3
    The Hedge Maze, 88–89
milk, 80–81. *See also coconut milk/cream*
    The Lamb's Tail, 90–91
    The Milky Moon, 8–9
mint, 6–7, 32–33, 64–65, 70–71
mixing glass, x
mixing methods, xv
muddler, xi

O

orange bitters, 24–25, 38–39
orange soda, 58–59
oranges/orange juice, 2–3, 54–55

P

peach liqueur, 6–7
pineapple juice, 4–5, 64–65

R

raspberries, 66–67, 78–79
Rhubarb Syrup, 66–67
root beer, 26–27
rose water, 56–57, 62–63

Rosemary Syrup, 22–23
rum, añejo
    The Calypso, 76–77
    The Lamb's Tail, 90–91
rum, gold
    The First Man, 28–29
    Milk of Gold, 86–87
    The Milky Moon, 8–9
    Nectar of the Gods, 62–63
rum, light
    Flower of Palms, 56–57
    Pith of Sticks, 18–19
    The Trifecta, 70–71
rum, white, 40–41

S

sage, 4–5
salt rim, creating, xiv
Salted Honey Syrup, 52–53, 62–63,
    74–75
Scotch
    The Bell Tower, 64–65
    The Flower Crown, 74–75
    The Pointed Leaf, 84–85
shakers, ix
sherry, 30–31, 38–39, 84–85
simple syrup, making, xiii
Smoked Black Tea Concentrate, 7
sparkling wine, 14–15, 32–33
strainers, x
strawberries, 10–11
syrups, xiii, 30–31, 42–43, 84–85
    Black Pepper Syrup, 10–11
    Brown Sugar Syrup, 32–33
    Cinnamon Syrup, 18–19, 56–57
    Cinnamon–Brown Sugar Syrup, 24–25
    Ginger-Chili Syrup, 16–17
    Honey Syrup, 14–15
    Rhubarb Syrup, 66–67
    Rosemary Syrup, 22–23
    Salted Honey Syrup, 52–53, 62–63,
        74–75

T

tarot, background of, vii–viii
tea, 8–9

The Flower Crown, 74–75
    Smoked Black Tea Concentrate, 6–7
techniques, xii–xv
tequila. *See also mezcal*
    Arc of Time, 34–35
    City of Emerald, 82–83
    The Mirage, 72–73
    Root of All, 26–27
    Spice of Life, 16–17
    The Sundial, 46–47
thyme, 34–35
tomato juice, 36–37
tools, ix–xi
triple sec, 46–47, 54–55
turmeric, 86–87

V

vanilla ice cream, 58–59
vermouth, dry, 44–45
vermouth, sweet
    The Mirage, 72–73
    Monk of the Mountains, 68–69
violet liqueur, 44–45
vodka
    Break of Dawn, 36–37
    Princess of Moscow, 20–21
    The Straw Man, 10–11

W

walnut bitters, 84–85
watermelon, 70–71
whiskey, rye
    The Feast, 24–25
    The Gold Standard, 52–53
wine, 12–13, 14–15, 32–33, 66–67

Andrews McMeel Publishing
a division of Andrews McMeel Universal
1130 Walnut Street, Kansas City, Missouri 64106

www.andrewsmcmeel.com

18 19 20 21 22 TEN 10 9 8 7 6 5 4 3 2 1

ISBN: 978-1-4494-8911-3

Library of Congress Control Number: 2018940590

Editor: Allison Adler
Art Director: Holly Swayne
Production Manager: Carol Coe
Production Editor: Dave Shaw

ATTENTION: SCHOOLS AND BUSINESSES

Andrews McMeel books are available at quantity discounts with bulk purchase for educational, business, or sales promotional use. For information, please e-mail the Andrews McMeel Publishing Special Sales Department: specialsales@amuniversal.com.